The Wealthy Diary Of

AFRICAN
WISDOM

A COLLECTION OF WISE AFRICAN PROVERBS,
CONVERSATIONS AND SHORT STORIES

CYNTHIA CHIRINDA

Wholeness
Publishing

The Wealthy Diary of African Wisdom
Copyright © 2016, 2025 by Cynthia Chirinda
First Published in 2016 by Wholeness Incorporated
Mass Media House, 19 Selous Avenue, Harare, Zimbabwe

E-mail: info@cynthiachirinda.com
Website: www.cynthiachirinda.com
Cover Design by Tapiwa Kahonde
Typesetting, Graphics and Layout: Tapiwa Kahonde
and Annie Nyamudzwadzuro

Unless otherwise stated, all Bible quotations are taken from the King James Version (KJV).

All rights reserved. No part of this publication may be reproduced, stored in a retrieval system, or transmitted in any form or by any means, without prior permission in writing from the publisher, nor be otherwise circulated in any form of binding or cover other than that in which it is published and without a similar condition including this condition being imposed on the subsequent purchaser.

ISBN: 978-0-7974-7210-5

Contents

The Wisdom Knot — v

Dedication — vii

Acknowledgements — ix

Preface — xi

Introduction — xiii

1: The Essence of Thought Leadership — 1

2: Values Based Ethical Leadership — 7

3: Women—Africa's greatest untapped resource — 13

4: The Power of Unity and the African Renaissance — 19

5: Trans-generational Thinking — 25

6: Innovation in Africa — 31

7: Transformational Leadership for Africa — 37

8: Unleashing Greatness — 43

9: The African Family Institution — 49

10: Roots and Wings — 55

11: The Power of Determination — 61

12: Conflict Resolution — 67

13: The Power of Focus — 73

14: Lasting Legacies — 79

15: Basking in Past Glory — 83

16: Divide and Rule — 87

17: The Power of the Tongue	91
18: What do You Answer to?	97
19: Strategic Thinking	103
20: The Power of Vulnerability	109
21: High Seat versus Low Seat Issues	115
22: So Rich yet So Poor	121
23: Making a Difference	127
24: Wisdom in Counsel	133
25: Love, Stability and Pandemics	139
26: Thinking before you Act	145
27: The Power of Community	151
28: Dysfunctions from over-dependency	157
29: The Cancer of Corruption	163
30: Greed and Selfishness	169
31: Sober Thinking	175
Final Word: A Call to the Sons and Daughters of Africa	181
About the Author	183

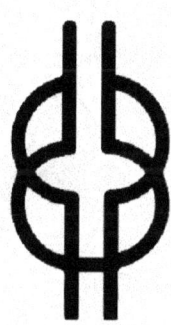

NYANSAPO—"Wisdom Knot"
Symbol of wisdom, ingenuity, intelligence and patience
This symbol conveys the idea that "a wise person has the capacity to choose the best means to attain a goal. Being wise implies broad knowledge, learning and experience, and the ability to apply such faculties to practical ends."

DEDICATION

To the courageous sons and daughters of Africa, whose selfless pursuit of trans-generational thinking and transformative leadership is shaping a developed Africa—one that we, and generations to come, will be proud to call home.

May this book serve as both mirror and compass to all who dare to lead, build, and become the change our continent so desperately needs.

Acknowledgements

I have been truly blessed to walk alongside wise mentors who share a passion for Africa's development. Among them are family, friends, spiritual leaders, ministry associates, and compatriots across the continent. I extend heartfelt gratitude to every man and woman whose encouragement along the journey inspired the writing of this book. Your voices have propelled me toward my significant calling and life purpose.

To each one who continues to believe in Africa's redemptive journey—thank you for walking with me.

PREFACE

There comes a time in life when one grows restless with the status quo—when our best efforts, thoughts, and expressions fall short of the impact we long to see. For years, I have carried a deep yearning: to see the dignity of Africa and her people not only restored, but reconstructed into a more glorious state—for the sake of her future sons and daughters.

When I wrote *Intelligent Conversations: A Mindset Shift Towards a Developed Africa* in 2014, my goal was to provoke thought leaders to arise and take their positions in bringing transformation to our continent. I longed to see a shift in mindset—where current leaders would mentor and accommodate a new generation of ethical visionaries. I wanted Africans to embrace their prophetic, spiritual assignment.

This expanded and refined edition comes at a critical juncture in Africa's development story. It reflects a deeper understanding, matured by time, fieldwork, and the lived experiences of change-makers across the continent.

In my interactions with fellow Africans, I realized many were unaware of the wealth that lies beneath the surface of our continent—beyond natural resources. Wisdom is deeply woven into our culture, words, and worldview. It is only perceived by those who believe in the hidden treasures of the intangible and are willing to listen beyond what is spoken.

The format of this book is designed as a diary, with thirty-one sections to facilitate daily meditation on African sayings, analysis of the embedded wisdom, and space for the reader to reflect, act, and grow. Each chapter is an invitation—not just to read, but to reflect, respond, and record your own journey of growth and purpose.

May these pages awaken your spirit, sharpen your vision, and embolden your steps as a steward of Africa's rebirth.

Introduction

If culture is a vital instrument of development, and language is the vessel that carries culture, then proverbs—our metaphorical treasures—deserve center stage in any conversation on development.

My childhood in deep rural Africa, though marked by challenges, became the fertile ground where my deepest life lessons took root. Listening to the elders and absorbing the layered meanings of their sayings taught me that wisdom often hides behind simple expressions. In school, I immersed myself in African literature, and I came to recognize how richly blessed I am to stand on the legacy of those who came before me.

Africa is endowed with incredible wealth—not just in minerals and beauty, but in her ancestral wisdom. From profound sayings about life, unity, and community to counsel on family, leadership, and patience, our proverbs offer a map for becoming a great people.

This book is a *Nyansapo*—a wisdom knot—inviting the reader to untie layers of insight, one proverb at a time. Proverbs remain central to our culture, passed from generation to generation as tools for teaching, celebrating, advising, and inspiring. As Chinua Achebe once said, "Proverbs are the palm oil with which words are eaten."

How much of this rare treasure have we truly applied to our development? Each new day brings an opportunity to rediscover this wealth. It is time for Africa's sons and daughters to awaken to their divine purpose—to rise with courage and create trans-generational solutions. This call is urgent. As we navigate valleys of turmoil and transition, Africa's authentic thought leaders must be roused like the dry bones in Ezekiel 37.

Arise, Sons and Daughters of Africa—uncover the wealth of wisdom in the generous bosom of Mother Africa!

The Wealthy Diary Of

AFRICAN
WISDOM

A Collection of Wise African Proverbs,
Conversations and Short Stories

CHAPTER ONE

THE ESSENCE OF THOUGHT LEADERSHIP

Proverb of the Day

"AN ARMY OF SHEEP LED BY A LION CAN DEFEAT AN ARMY OF LIONS LED BY A SHEEP."

African Proverb

Insights into Thought Leadership

Thought leadership is a common term in the business world. To the average person, however, it may come across as just another corporate buzzword. But behind the jargon lies an honest and admirable ambition: to be viewed as a credible, trusted voice—someone who cuts through the noise and offers wisdom that matters.

In essence, thought leaders are people of impact who invest in themselves—not out of selfishness, but with the intention of enhancing their ability to serve, produce, and contribute meaningfully. These individuals change the world in lasting ways and inspire others to join them by offering best practices, frameworks, and models of sustainable action. They build foundations for others to grow upon, without a possessive grip on their ideas.

One need only look to the legacies of African giants like Nelson Mandela or Wangari Maathai to witness how visionary leadership can birth movements that transcend individual achievement.

Conversations on Thought Leadership

"Thought leadership ought to occupy the core of strategy in any unit or organisation and thereby become the leading proposition that brings organised, principled structure, innovation and direction for the common good. It is a tragedy that whilst thought leadership carries so much hope and promise, there is more that militates against the rise of thought leaders in African societies than there is to promote them. Thought leaders are people of impact who go beyond offering much needed expertise across ecosystems but possess the ability to elevate and inspire people with innovative ideas. Thought leaders have the unique ability to transform ideas into tangible reality, and demonstrate wisdom in replicating their success. They work with and through other individuals who provide assistance with the common goal of ensuring that every success is replicated on various levels and frame those ideas into sustainable change beyond micro-systems but across entire ecosystems and life spans."

—©2014 Cynthia Chirinda, *Intelligent Conversations: A Mindset Shift towards a Developed Africa*

In his inaugural professorial lecture at UNISA in 2014, Professor Vusi Gumede expanded on the power and imperative of thought leadership:

"The African continent remains at crossroads. The world as a whole remains uncertain, volatile, dangerous and indeed unjust. This is an indictment to the global human society as a whole. To better the human condition, to further advance Africa's development, and to bring about a just world, we need (1) Thought leadership; (2) Thought liberation; and (3) Critical consciousness. A combination of these three ingredients, arguably, should make for a better world to live in—and indeed a better Africa to leave behind for the future generations. Thought leadership without critical consciousness is useless. Thought leadership without a liberated mind is futile. Higher levels of consciousness, based on comprehensive understanding of phenomena, make for a better thought leader. And, if that thought leader is also mentally liberated and psychosocially free, undoubtedly Africa shall be free and the world would, in time, be a great place to live in.

The central importance of thought leadership to Africa's renewal and development is unquestionable and compelling, especially in view of the low and peripheral position that the African continent occupies in the global political, social and economic order. The dominance of foreign thoughts in the conceptualisation and implementation of developmental and other policies, the inevitable abysmal failure of such thoughts to bring about the much needed transformation in Africa and the world at large, the entrapment of African leadership and citizenry by such thoughts make thought liberation an inescapable imperative. The low levels of (critical) consciousness ensure, sadly, that Africa and Africans remain in chains, hence the case for higher levels of critical consciousness."

— *Vusi Gumede, "Thought Leadership, Thought Liberation, and Critical Consciousness for Africa's Development and a Just World," PhD Inaugural Professorial Lecture, 19 March 2014, Senate Hall, UNISA*

These insights call us to reflect not only on what we know, but how we use that knowledge to liberate others and co-create a just future for Africa. Thought leadership is not just a position—it is a responsibility to carry truth, vision, and courage into spaces that long for transformation.

Transformative Actions: My Commitment and Contribution

≈ I commit to being a vessel of clarity, truth, and innovation in every space I occupy.
≈ I will cultivate my inner world so that my outer influence carries wisdom, not just words.
≈ I choose to serve not for recognition, but to leave behind frameworks, footprints, and fertile ground for others to flourish.
≈ I will think deeply, act boldly, and lead responsibly—because Africa's future depends on the quality of our thought leaders today.

Now it's your turn:

- What space in your life is calling for courageous thought leadership?
- What idea, insight, or wisdom can you offer your community that leads toward renewal and justice?

NOTES
TRANSFORMATIVE ACTIONS: MY COMMITMENT AND CONTRIBUTION

CHAPTER TWO

VALUES BASED ETHICAL LEADERSHIP

Proverb of the Day

"A CLEAR CONSCIENCE MAKES A SOFT PILLOW."

African Proverb

Values-Based Ethical Leadership and the African Moral System

Values are the standards that guide our actions, judgments, and attitudes. They represent the qualities, characteristics, or ideals we feel strongly about. Our values define what is of worth, what is beneficial, and what is harmful. They affect our decisions, shape our goals, and influence our behavior.

Moral values are the standards of good and evil that govern an individual's behavior and choices. These may derive from various sources: society, government, religion, or personal conscience. When moral values are rooted in societal norms or laws, they tend to shift with changing cultural climates. However, ethics go deeper—they pertain to moral principles that help us discern right from wrong, and offer a compass for navigating personal and public life. While some may assume morality is purely private, the idea of "private morality" is essentially contradictory.

While Africa is rich in natural and human resources, many nations across the continent continue to grapple with poverty and underdevelopment. Corruption, multinational plundering, and poor management of resources are among the greatest challenges. Leaders bear the responsibility to model ethical standards, to articulate and uphold them, and to maintain personal integrity in public service. Establishing a culture of values and ethical behavior must be integral to leadership development within institutions and nations alike.

It is possible to coach good leaders into becoming great leaders—those who lead with clarity, consistency, and a deep sense of purpose. Many developed nations have successfully created ethical leadership frameworks to guide individuals and organizations. In contrast, Africans have often undervalued their indigenous models, preferring imported ethics over their own. Yet Africa's traditional value systems, rooted in proverbial wisdom and cultural teachings, offer timeless principles that remain deeply relevant even amidst social and technological change.

Good character is the essence of the African moral system—the linchpin of ethical living. While society can impart moral knowledge, it is character that determines whether individuals live by those principles. African societies pass on their ethics through stories, folktales, and proverbs that embed values in daily life. But knowing what is right is not the same as doing what is right. Thus, moral education must be paired with a lived commitment to character development.

Within any organization, values guide decision-making and define what is important for success. They express what an organization stands for and direct the behavior of its people. Ethics, meanwhile, provide a standard for determining appropriate or moral conduct. The ethics of a society are reflected in its conceptions of justice, harmony, good character, and communal living. In African societies, ethics are deeply woven into community life, and articulated by moral thinkers, elders, and cultural custodians.

The Magnificent Seven Principles

The present cannot be separated from the past. Africa's political values have historically emphasized nationalism and cultural identity, but often lack strong pillars in accountability, honesty, and prioritization of the common good. When corruption thrives, it signifies a breakdown in honesty. When natural resources are exploited by external actors, it points to a lack of self-worth and self-governance. Inefficiency, in many cases, is the byproduct of ego and outdated leadership models.

To counter this, seven universal values can anchor ethical decision-making. These are:
1. **Dignity of Human Life**
2. **Autonomy**
3. **Honesty**
4. **Loyalty**
5. **Fairness**
6. **Humaneness**
7. **The Common Good**

These values serve as a moral compass for leaders across all levels. Yet, the challenge is not whether people claim these values—but whether they live them. The gap between what is preached and what is practiced is often wide.

Transformative Actions: My Commitment and Contribution

≈ I commit to leading with integrity in both private and public spaces.
≈ I will examine my decisions and actions through the lens of values that uplift, unify, and dignify others.
≈ I will honor Africa's indigenous ethics—not as relics of the past, but as resilient wisdom for present and future leadership.
≈ I choose to be a mirror of the leadership I want to see—accountable, honest, and rooted in purpose.
≈ Leadership is not a title—it is a daily ethical choice.

Now it's your turn:

- Are your personal and professional decisions aligned with the values you profess?
- What one value will you intentionally uphold this week—no matter the cost?

NOTES
TRANSFORMATIVE ACTIONS: MY COMMITMENT AND CONTRIBUTION

Chapter Three

Women—Africa's Greatest Untapped Resource

Proverb of the Day

"WHEN YOU EDUCATE A MAN YOU EDUCATE AN INDIVIDUAL; WHEN YOU EDUCATE A WOMAN, YOU EDUCATE A GENERATION."

African Proverb

The Empowerment of Women is Key to African Development

In recent decades, Africa has ranked among the fastest-growing economies globally. Economic analyses—such as those published in the *Harvard Business Review*—have pointed to the rapid rise in African consumer markets and entrepreneurial activity. Yet, this growth has not proportionately benefitted women.

Women are the backbone of developing communities. This is especially true across Africa, where women reinvest up to 90% of their income into their families and communities—compared to just 30–40% by men. Despite this, women remain on the periphery of economic and political power.

Conversations on the Pivotal Role of Women in Africa's Development

"The key question is whether Africa's economic growth can be sustained when so much of it is based on extractive resources—and whether it can make a significant dent in inequality that leaves so many behind. The answer is a qualified 'yes'; but only if we build our economies on a solid foundation. That foundation requires the unleashing of the tamped down energy, resourcefulness, and power of Africa's women and girls.

Women and girls are Africa's greatest untapped resource. It is they—not diamonds, oil, or minerals—who will serve as the foundation for sustainable and equitable progress. Expanding the freedoms, education, and opportunities of women holds the key to inclusive economic growth. This is true worldwide, and especially true in Africa."

—Joaquim Chissano, Former President of Mozambique, Excerpt from Europe's World, February 2014

Raising Transformational Female Leaders

In Africa, women constitute more than half of the population. Yet, two-thirds remain illiterate, and their political representation still lags behind global averages. Women make up less than 30% of global parliamentary participation. While they form a dominant part of society—and half the electorate—their influence on policy and decision-making remains limited.

Women were not created as an afterthought. They were intentionally designed by the Creator to exercise dominion, nurture life, and co-steward the earth. They are not only incubators of life but also of ideas, vision, and transformation.

It is imperative that we deliberately invest in developing women's leadership capacities from a young age. When we train girls to think critically, speak courageously, and lead ethically, we begin to sow the seeds of national transformation.

What Makes Women Great Leaders?

- **They value work–life balance.**
  Women excel in integrating personal and professional roles with wisdom and grace.
- **They are empathetic.**
  With strong relational instincts, they understand motivation, emotion, and the importance of human connection.

- **They are exceptional listeners.**
  Rather than rushing to react, women take time to listen deeply and respond intentionally.
- **They are nurturing.**
  Great leadership involves developing others. Women naturally support the growth and success of those around them.
- **They are strong communicators.**
  Communication is one of women's most powerful leadership tools—used with clarity, connection, and confidence.
- **They possess high emotional intelligence.**
  Women often lead with empathy, discernment, and self-awareness—key traits in emotionally intelligent leadership.
- **They are collaborative multi-taskers.**
  Women navigate complexity with grace, juggling roles and building inclusive coalitions.
- **They are courageous questioners.**
  Given safe space, women explore with depth, courage, and critical insight.
- **They are opportunity-driven.**
  In every challenge, women often see a window for growth, resilience, and reinvention.
- **They are passionate explorers.**
  Often misunderstood as overly emotional, women's passion fuels excellence and innovation.
- **They are entrepreneurial by nature.**
  Women harness resourcefulness, build relationships, and turn ideas into enterprises.

The best women leaders possess circular vision—balancing emotional intelligence, strategic foresight, and ethical stewardship. When women lead, communities thrive.

Africa's transformation hinges not only on external investments or policy reform, but on the elevation of its women. The future demands that we recognize women as core architects of progress and stewards of generational wisdom.

Transformative Actions: My Commitment and Contribution

- ≈ I commit to creating platforms where women's voices are not only heard—but heeded.
- ≈ I will mentor emerging female leaders with intentionality, believing in their capacity to carry nations forward.
- ≈ I will challenge systems and cultures that silence, suppress, or sideline women.
- ≈ I will honour the women who came before me by empowering the girls who come after me.

Africa's reformation depends on the restoration of her women.

Now it's your turn

- In what ways can you advocate for or support the elevation of women in your community, workplace, or nation?
- How can you nurture and champion the untapped greatness of a woman or girl in your sphere today?

NOTES
TRANSFORMATIVE ACTIONS: MY COMMITMENT AND CONTRIBUTION

Chapter Four

THE POWER OF UNITY AND THE AFRICAN RENAISSANCE

Proverb of the Day

"CHARA CHIMWE HACHITSWANYI INDA." (SHONA)
"ONE THUMB CANNOT CRUSH A LOUSE."

Zimbabwean Proverb

African Unity: The Cornerstone of the African Renaissance

The African Renaissance is more than a philosophical ideal. It is a call for **social cohesion, democratic renewal, economic rebirth, and Africa's rightful place in global affairs**. Yet this vision cannot be actualized without unity. African unity is not a romantic dream; it is a practical imperative.

The journey toward continental awakening demands the transformation of inherited institutions and the re-imagination of development frameworks. A reorientation toward **thought leadership**, the reversal of brain drain, and the intentional amplification of African voices must sit at the heart of this vision.

Africans must look beyond tribal, national, and ideological divides to embrace a shared identity. We must move from competition to collaboration, from fragmentation to federation. Only then can the African Renaissance move from rhetoric to reality.

Conversations on the African Renaissance

The *Abuja Treaty* of 1991 laid the groundwork for continental unity through the establishment of the African Economic Community. This visionary treaty outlined a **34-year program of regional integration**, encouraging economic communities to evolve into free trade areas, customs unions, and, ultimately, a continental common market.

Earlier still, the *Organisation of African Unity (OAU)*—founded in 1963—pioneered efforts in cross-regional cooperation, uniting African nations in foreign policy, science and technology, education, and economic collaboration. These early institutions planted seeds of unity rooted in shared purpose and collective benefit.

Today, the *African Union* and its developmental framework—*The New Partnership for Africa's Development (NEPAD)*—represent the continuation of this dream. But declarations must be met with determined implementation. **Unity must translate into infrastructure**, governance, education, and innovation systems that are inclusive and future-focused.

Thought Leadership for Implementation

The vision of unity must confront the **reality of disarticulation**—where the theory of integration often outpaces the practice of it. As *Zukiswa Mqolomba* writes:

> *"The programme of the African Renaissance should be expected to play an important frontline role in the decade ahead... Greater thought leadership is required to respond to the seeming disarticulation between theory and the empirical."*

Bridging this gap requires a **new breed of leaders**: principled, visionary, and rooted in pan-African consciousness. These leaders must move swiftly—not just to theorize—but to build systems that serve, heal, and empower.

We are at a tipping point.

Unity is no longer a poetic aspiration. It is a strategic necessity.

And the time to rise—together—is now.

Transformative Actions: My Commitment and Contribution

- ≈ I commit to championing unity not just in rhetoric, but in practice.
- ≈ I will pursue collaboration over competition, and cross-sector synergy over siloed agendas.
- ≈ I will use my platforms to amplify the call for pan-African cooperation—rooted in shared identity and visionary leadership.
- ≈ I will bridge the gap between promise and practice by contributing to systems that are inclusive, ethical, and future-oriented.

Now it's your turn:

- What does African unity mean to you—personally and professionally?
- How can you promote connection and collaboration across your sphere of influence?

NOTES
TRANSFORMATIVE ACTIONS: MY COMMITMENT AND CONTRIBUTION

CHAPTER FIVE

TRANS-GENERATIONAL THINKING

Proverb of the Day

"FOR TOMORROW BELONGS TO THE PEOPLE WHO PREPARE FOR IT TODAY."

— African Proverb

Buying the Future: The Call to Trans-generational Vision

Across Africa, leaders are rising to redirect the continent toward agency, sovereignty, and sustainable development. Yet to truly shift Africa's destiny, a deeper reorientation is required—one rooted in **trans-generational thinking**.

This is a season of prophetic responsibility—where we must not only cast vision, but invest in futures we may never personally occupy. Africa's redemption will be shaped not only by its present efforts, but by its leaders' capacity to **think beyond the now**, **serve beyond the self**, and **plant trees whose shade they may never sit under**.

Stirring a New Kind of Conversation

As an African woman grounded in spiritual calling and systems thinking, I've watched many conversations take place in conference rooms, boardrooms, and policy circles. And yet I often ask: *What will these conversations serve at the table of Africa?* Will they nourish the next generation—or recycle survival strategies masked as vision?

We need conversations that stir hearts and challenge mental models—**conversations that call individuals out of passive spectatorship into active participation** in Africa's becoming. We must each ask:

- *What seeds am I sowing that future generations will harvest?*

- *What legacy am I crafting—intentionally or by default?*
- *Am I buying the future—or merely renting the present?*

The Inner Work of Personal Leadership

Trans-generational vision is not abstract—it begins with **personal leadership**. As transformational leaders, we must cultivate the ability to regulate ourselves, articulate our purpose, and walk in alignment with calling.

We cannot demand from institutions what we have not yet demanded from ourselves. Leaders of impact are those who live with clarity and conviction, guided by the foundational questions of personal leadership:

- Who am I?
- Why am I here?
- Where am I going?
- How will I get there?
- What will be my legacy?

These questions are not once-off reflections. They are **living compasses**, recalibrated over time by wisdom, failure, mentorship, and divine guidance.

Buying the Future: Lessons from Dr. Mensa Otabil

In his powerful teaching series *Buy the Future*, Dr. Mensa Otabil paints a picture of the generational thinker—one who sows seeds today that others may harvest tomorrow. He writes:

> *"Buying the future is synonymous with achieving development goals."*

This truth applies to individuals, families, institutions, and nations. Visionary figures such as Bill Gates and Aliko Dangote have shaped economies not just by their presence, but by their foresight—their audacity to create long-term solutions to generational problems.

Transformative Actions: My Commitment and Contribution

- ≈ I commit to being a trans-generational thinker—one who sows not for applause, but for legacy.
- ≈ I will mentor the next generation with intention, invest in long-term solutions, and create blueprints that outlive me.
- ≈ I will resist the pull of short-termism and embrace the sacred work of planting seeds I may never see bloom.

Now it's your turn:

- What are *you* doing today to buy the future?
- How will your actions today build bridges for generations yet to come? Africa needs builders—not just for today, but for tomorrow's cities. Africa needs mentors—not only for the youth we see, but for the generations we will never meet.
  Trans-generational thought leadership is the bridge from our pain to our promise.

NOTES - TRANSFORMATIVE ACTIONS: MY COMMITMENT AND CONTRIBUTION

Chapter Six

INNOVATION IN AFRICA

Proverb of the Day

"ZVINHU ZVIEDZWA, CHEMBERE YEKWACHIVI
YAKABIKA MABWE YAKASEVA MUTO."

(LITERAL TRANSLATION: THINGS ARE TO BE TRIED, AN OLD LADY
COOKED STONES AND THEY PRODUCED SOUP).

Zimbabwean Proverb

A True Story of Innovation Stifled

In 1997, Dr. Ezekiel Izuogu, a brilliant Igbo electrical engineer and lecturer at the Federal Polytechnic Nekede, designed and developed the Izuogu Z-600—the first African-made car designed and manufactured locally. Nicknamed "the African dream machine" by the BBC, the Z-600 was 90% locally sourced and poised to become the most affordable car in the world, with a projected cost of only $2,000.

With mass production planned at Izuogu Motors in Naze, Owerri, the car could have launched an industrial revolution in Nigeria. The Z-600 featured a self-made 1.8L four-cylinder engine, achieving 18mpg and speeds of up to 140 km/h. The design prioritized front-wheel drive to reduce production costs, and the car passed the Nigerian federal government's inquiry with only minor cosmetic recommendations.

But despite promises of support and a pledged grant of 235 million naira, no funding was ever released. In 2006, just as Dr. Izuogu was preparing to relocate production to South Africa at the government's invitation, his factory was looted. Moulds, engine blocks, design notebooks, and other key materials were stolen, effectively killing the dream. More than monetary loss, it was a national tragedy—a theft of intellectual capital and possibility.

Conversations on Innovation in Africa

This story underscores the systemic barriers to innovation on the continent. While there are signs of a growing innovation culture in some regions, numerous factors continue to impede progress:

1. Dependency on Aid

Decades of well-meaning foreign aid have weakened self-determination. Innov—ation is stifled when solutions are dictated externally. Aid, when not empowering or contextualized, risks becoming a new form of colonialism.

2. Obsolete Educational Systems

Many African schools still lack curricula that encourage creativity or teach problem-solving and design thinking. Without a strong STEM foundation, the pipeline for homegrown engineers, inventors, and entrepreneurs remains narrow. Curricula reform has begun in some regions, but scale and depth remain inadequate.

3. Survivalist Mindsets and Risk Aversion

A "survival mode" mentality, often inherited from generations of economic insecurity, leads many young Africans to prioritize secure jobs over bold, entrepreneurial ventures. This stifles creativity and long-term investment in innovation.

Beyond Barriers: What's Needed for Breakthrough

Innovation in Africa cannot be left to individual genius alone—it must be structurally cultivated. The continent's challenges are complex and interconnected, demanding interdisciplinary, systemic approaches. Governments, schools, families, and private sectors must collaborate to:

- Cultivate opportunity-based entrepreneurship rather than necessity-driven survivalism.
- Revise national education frameworks to encourage innovation, experimentation, and failure as a learning tool.

- Invest in African-led incubators and funding models for early-stage ventures.
- Promote intellectual property rights and safeguard local innovation.

Africa doesn't lack brilliance—it lacks enabling environments.

Transformative Actions: My Commitment and Contribution

As a peacebuilder and practitioner grounded in systems change, **I commit to**:

≈ Curating spaces where African innovators can reflect, reframe, and reimagine futures without fear.
≈ Facilitating workshops that combine traditional wisdom and modern design thinking.
≈ Supporting the development of youth incubators that foster transdisciplinary innovation.
≈ Continuing to write, teach, and advocate for an Africa that not only remembers its stories of ingenuity—but writes new ones.

Let us remember the dreams that were buried and become the midwives of those yet to be born.

Now it's your turn:

What does innovation look like in your community or sphere of influence? What step can you take to empower a local solution, an unheard voice, or a new idea?

NOTES
TRANSFORMATIVE ACTIONS: MY COMMITMENT AND CONTRIBUTION

CHAPTER SEVEN

TRANSFORMATIONAL LEADERSHIP FOR AFRICA

Proverb of the Day

A GREAT LEADER IS AN ORDINARY PERSON WITH EXTRAORDINARY WISDOM.

Malawian Proverb

Reframing Leadership for a New Africa

Leadership is not only about knowledge, skills, and competencies. It is deeply shaped by worldviews—our values, principles, and beliefs about what is right, just, and possible. These internal lenses act as filters: they determine how we see ourselves, how we engage others, and how we shape systems. When applied with intentionality, worldviews become frameworks for transformation, guiding not only what leaders do—but how they do it and why.

In Africa, the need for leaders who operate from transformational worldviews is urgent. Our cultural default often leans toward **transactional leadership**—a style rooted in exchange, reward, and punishment. It prioritizes compliance over creativity and immediate results over long-term restoration. While such leadership may deliver short-term order, it rarely births lasting transformation.

By contrast, **transformational leadership** cultivates meaning and motivation. It focuses on influence through vision, character, and care. Transformational leaders inspire others to pursue purpose, align with shared values, and bring their best selves to the work at hand—not for a reward, but from a deeper sense of ownership and calling.

They recognize strengths, assign wisely, nurture growth, and invite people into a journey of shared transformation. In doing so, they don't just lead tasks—they raise leaders.

Conversations on Transformational Leadership in Africa

"Africa today is an eagle that is yet to soar. She needs to tell herself that she is an eagle who belongs to the sky. Every imagination that places Africa in a lower category in relation to other peoples should be replaced with new thoughts that see Africa at the center stage in global development.

The greatest challenge to Africa's development is the mind of Africans. African minds should be transformed into new minds that can release a new Africa into existence. Africa needs leaders who have faith as well as the ability to translate their good faith into good works.

The time to rethink is now! The time for new resolves is now! The time for new action is now! May Africa soar to new heights like super eagles!"

—Dr. Delanyo Adadevoh, *Leading Transformation in Africa*

Transformational Roots in Family and Ubuntu

Africa does not need to import the values of transformational leadership—it already holds them in its cultural DNA. The principle of **Ubuntu**, grounded in familial structures and community interdependence, is one of the most powerful and enduring expressions of African leadership.

Ubuntu emphasizes human dignity, connectedness, and compassion. It reminds us that we are because others are. Leadership, in this sense, is not about position or power—it is about relational stewardship.

The family unit, often overlooked in formal leadership discourse, is one of the most fertile environments for developing these values. Here, children learn to negotiate, empathize, listen, take responsibility, and serve. These foundational skills are the building blocks of emotional intelligence and relational leadership.

As research continues to show, the most impactful leaders today are those who can **manage relationships**, cultivate trust, and lead with emotional and cultural intelligence. And these are precisely the strengths that the African family—when whole—can nurture.

Call to Action: Shaping Leaders with Vision

Africa stands at the edge of its next chapter, and the call is clear: we need **leaders who see farther**, dream bolder, and serve deeper.

We need leaders who are not merely trained—but transformed.

Leaders who embody humility, conviction, and wisdom.

Leaders who can look a generation ahead and design systems that endure.

The transformational leadership we long for in our governments, organizations, churches, and communities must begin with the **transformed individual**.

This is not a far-off ideal—it is a present possibility.

My Transformative Actions: My Commitment and Contribution

≈ Intentionally invest in mentoring and leadership formation rooted in values, integrity, and service.
≈ Integrate Ubuntu-inspired leadership principles into civic and organizational training models.
≈ Host dialogue spaces where leaders reflect on their own worldviews and leadership motivations.
≈ Model transformational leadership through consistent relational stewardship, presence, and strategic visioning.

Now it's your turn:

- What transformative actions will you commit to in your leadership journey?
- What mindsets or practices must you shift to become the leader Africa needs?

NOTES
TRANSFORMATIVE ACTIONS: MY COMMITMENT AND CONTRIBUTION

CHAPTER EIGHT

UNLEASHING GREATNESS

Proverb of the Day

"THE GREAT TREE CHOOSES WHERE TO GROW AND
WE FIND IT THERE, SO IT IS WITH
THE GREATNESS IN MEN."

African Proverb

Unleashing Greatness

What is greatness, and how do people arrive there?

Is it a matter of destiny or design, talent or tenacity?

Few questions have stirred as much debate, fascination, and reflection. From ancient traditions to modern societies, the heights of human accomplishment have always captivated the imagination. We long to know—what makes someone great?

In earlier times, greatness was seen as divine—bestowed by the gods or woven into the fabric of fate. Today, we increasingly recognize greatness as a product of persistent vision, cultivated skill, and courageous choice. Still, greatness continues to elude simple definition. It cannot be confined to titles, fame, or wealth. True greatness is deeply relational—it serves, uplifts, and inspires others.

Conversations on Unleashing Africa's Greatness

Africa, too, is destined for greatness. But destiny alone is not enough. It must be awakened by belief and activated by bold, transformative action.

Africans must begin to believe again—

To believe in their power to shape the future.

To believe that broken systems can be rebuilt.

To believe that the wisdom of our ancestors and the creativity of our youth can co-create a new era.

This belief, however, cannot live in isolation. It must be nurtured by leadership that empowers others, challenges the status quo, and invites intelligent conversations that birth innovative solutions. We need leaders who see beyond personal ambition—those who recognize that **every African is a potential agent of change.**

To sustain and accelerate Africa's progress, we must move from insight to implementation. We must cultivate partnerships across government, business, civil society, and the diaspora—working together toward shared objectives of economic growth and social transformation.

As Dr. Bernard Nwaka, a Zambian faith leader and servant-leadership advocate has so aptly said:

"Greatness does not come from occupying great seats of power but in serving the people."

Indeed, greatness is not measured by what we possess, but by what we give.

It is found not in status, but in service.

Not in accumulation, but in contribution.

When we engage in courageous, intelligent conversations—and take personal and collective responsibility for our growth—we unleash the greatness that has always been within us.

Transformative Actions: My Commitment and Contribution

≈ I commit to nurturing greatness not just in myself, but in others.
≈ I will use my platforms to spark vision, my voice to call forth purpose, and my leadership to uplift communities.
≈ Africa's greatness is not a future hope—it is a present responsibility. I choose to rise.

Now it's your turn:

- What does greatness mean to you?
- What step can you take today to unlock the greatness within yourself—and within your community?

NOTES
TRANSFORMATIVE ACTIONS: MY COMMITMENT AND CONTRIBUTION

CHAPTER NINE

THE AFRICAN FAMILY INSTITUTION

Proverb of the Day

"A FAMILY IS LIKE A FOREST, WHEN YOU ARE OUTSIDE IT IS DENSE, WHEN YOU ARE INSIDE YOU SEE THAT EACH TREE HAS ITS PLACE."

African Proverb

Conversations on the African Family Institution: The Primacy of Family in African Philosophical Thought

The family is more than a social unit—it is the heartbeat of African society. It is the first government, the first school, the first economy, and the first sanctuary of spiritual and moral formation. In African cultural heritage, the family stands as the foundation upon which nations are built and sustained.

African philosophical thought affirms that cultivating family ethics—values such as love, loyalty, generosity, obedience, sincerity, and mutual care—sets the moral compass for broader society. When these virtues are nurtured within families, they ripple outward to transform communities, institutions, and nations.

At the heart of this philosophy is the principle of *familism*—a cultural ethos that emphasizes mutual belonging, shared responsibility, and intergenerational continuity. As **J.A. Sofola (1973)** describes in *African Culture and the African Personality*, familism is expressed through:

- A deep sense of belonging to the family group
- Integration of efforts toward collective goals
- Generosity toward members in need
- Rallying support in times of crisis

- Sustaining continuity between the ancestral and emerging family branches

The traditional African extended family embodies this ideal. It includes not only parents and children but also grandparents, uncles, aunts, cousins, and in-laws. It is a cooperative unit where each member contributes to the common good. The able support the vulnerable, and dignity is preserved even in the face of hardship.

This cooperative ethic is a countercultural treasure in a world driven by hyper-individualism and competition. Familism offers a redemptive paradigm—an antidote to the loneliness, consumerism, and fragmentation plaguing modern life. It is Africa's gift to a world in search of connectedness and meaning.

Furthermore, the African family institution plays a central role in governance and leadership formation. It is where people first learn to love, to serve, to resolve conflict, to honour authority, and to care for others. It is the training ground for the kind of ethical leadership that Africa so desperately needs.

To rebuild Africa, we must begin at home. The family must be protected, revalued, and resourced—not only as a cultural relic but as a strategic foundation for sustainable development, national unity, and peace.

Transformative Actions: My Commitment and Contribution

≈ I commit to restoring the dignity and strength of the African family.
≈ I will honour intergenerational wisdom, champion family-centered leadership, and create programs that uplift and support holistic family wellbeing.
≈ From my home to the nations, I choose to build from the inside out.

Now it's your turn:

- How can you invest in the strength of your family or community?
- What family value do you want to pass on to the next generation?

NOTES
TRANSFORMATIVE ACTIONS: MY COMMITMENT AND CONTRIBUTION

Chapter Ten

ROOTS AND WINGS

Proverb of the Day

"WE DESIRE TO BEQUEATH TWO THINGS TO OUR CHILDREN; THE FIRST ONE IS ROOTS, THE OTHER ONE IS WINGS."

Sudanese Proverb

The Power of Legacy

We live in a world filled with uncertainty and overstimulation—where fear often eclipses freedom, and caution outweighs curiosity. In this climate, too many children are raised "in captivity"—their behavior micromanaged, their potential doubted, and their wings clipped before they've had the chance to stretch.

And yet, the timeless wisdom of this African proverb reminds us: to raise children well is to give them both **roots** and **wings**.

Roots provide belonging, grounding, and heritage. They are about identity and memory, about knowing who you are and where you come from.

Wings symbolize freedom, vision, and possibility. They are about movement and exploration, about soaring into one's divine calling and uncharted future.

Personal Reflections on Roots and Wings

When I think of *roots*, I see a foundation of faith, family, culture, and character. I want my sons and daughters to be rooted not in fear or shame, but in love, identity, and divine truth. I want them to know their place in a long line of strength—the resilience of African mothers, the dignity of African fathers, the wisdom of ancestral voices.

A relationship with God the Creator is the deepest root I can nurture in their lives. And so, my home becomes the sacred soil—a space where love is constant, truth is spoken, prayers are lifted, and values are lived.

But as vital as roots are, *wings* are equally essential.

I want my children to soar. To think beyond borders. To explore, create, contribute, and fly. I want them to rise above limiting beliefs and societal ceilings. I want them to dance with wonder, walk with courage, and speak with clarity. Their wings are strengthened by permission—permission to question, to grow, to integrate their African wisdom with global insight, and to lead boldly with both.

Exhortation of the Day

What legacy are we shaping for the next generation?

Are we handing them more than survival skills—are we giving them soaring skills?

What language are you speaking into the hearts of the children in your care—does it root them in heritage and launch them toward destiny?

Are you nurturing both identity and imagination?

Africa's future does not begin in boardrooms—it begins in living rooms. It begins at bedtime stories and morning devotions, shared meals and sacred traditions. This is where the roots are grown. This is where the wings begin to stir.

Transformative Actions: My Commitment and Contribution

- ≈ I commit to being both a root-builder and a wing-giver.
- ≈ I will cultivate spaces where the next generation feels deeply grounded in their identity and wildly free to explore their destiny.
- ≈ I choose to raise legacy-makers—firm in truth, fierce in purpose, and free to fly.

Now it's your turn

- Who are the young people in your life, community, or nation you are called to root and release?
- What one action can you take today to nourish their foundation—and strengthen their wings?

NOTES
TRANSFORMATIVE ACTIONS: MY COMMITMENT AND CONTRIBUTION

Chapter Eleven

The Power of Determination

Proverb of the Day

"IF YOU ARE BUILDING A HOUSE AND A NAIL BREAKS, DO YOU STOP BUILDING OR DO YOU CHANGE THE NAIL?"

Rwandan Proverb

The Unyielding Spirit

Determination is the silent strength behind every legacy. It is what keeps us climbing when the mountain grows steeper, and what anchors us when the winds of adversity blow. It is the unseen fuel that distinguishes those who press through impossibility from those who settle comfortably in the valley of mediocrity.

In recent years, I've been reflecting deeply on what it means to remain determined in the face of resistance. Life rarely cooperates with our plans. It throws distractions, delays, and disappointments in our path. And if we're not careful, the fire of our dreams can slowly dim. Goals can shift. Vision can fade. Hope can retreat.

But we are not called to retreat.

Africa's Call for Determined Builders

When I look across our beloved continent, I see both beauty and brokenness. And I ask: *Who will stay the course when systems fail? Who will rebuild when the nails break? Who will pick up the tools again when others abandon the work?*

Too often, I sense that some have given up on the African dream—not because it is impossible, but because it is demanding. But Africa does not need more resignation. It needs resurrection—of hope, of vision, of unwavering determination.

Ours is a continent that has weathered storms and birthed civilizations. Now more than ever, we need a generation that will rise—not just to adapt to global shifts, but to **change the game**.

Game Changers Needed

The world is evolving at a rapid pace—technologically, socially, politically. And amid this evolution is a clarion call for individuals who do more than keep up. We need visionaries who reimagine, rebuild, and rewrite the story.

A game changer doesn't just respond to trends—they create new paths. They challenge stagnation. They carry innovation in one hand and service in the other. Their determination is not self-serving—it is generational.

Africa's transformation depends on such leaders—those who refuse to give up when the system resists, those who rise again when hope seems lost, and those who carry through the mission until the crown is reached.

Exhortation of the Day

What assignment have you abandoned because of broken nails and broken systems?

You were not created to miscarry your mission. You were designed to *carry through* to completion.

Your destiny is not just yours—it is tied to many. To give up now is to silence the song of generations yet unborn.

Refuse to quit. Refuse to bow. Refuse to leave the house unfinished.

The crown is not at the halfway point—it waits at the finish line.

Transformative Actions: My Commitment and Contribution

≈ I commit to remaining steadfast in my divine assignment, even when the tools are few and the terrain is tough.
≈ I will rebuild when others retreat. I will create new models when old systems fail.
≈ I choose to be a game changer—not for fame, but for future generations.

Now it's your turn:

- What vision have you abandoned that needs to be revived?
- What nail broke—and what new strategy can you pick up to keep building?

NOTES
TRANSFORMATIVE ACTIONS: MY COMMITMENT AND CONTRIBUTION

Chapter Twelve

Conflict Resolution

Proverb of the Day

"WHEN BROTHERS FIGHT TO THE DEATH, A STRANGER INHERITS THEIR FATHER'S ESTATE."

Igbo Proverb

The High Cost of Division

Africa's greatest tragedies are not always born out of scarcity—but out of **strife**.

At the heart of many of our most painful national and community wounds lies a failure to resolve conflict—not because solutions were unavailable, but because pride, power, and personal ambition were prioritized over people.

A deficit in **ethical and visionary leadership** continues to fracture our societies. Across the continent, we see the lingering consequences of unresolved tensions:

- Human rights violations
- Dysfunctional governance
- Electoral fraud and ethnic manipulation
- Corruption and self-enrichment by elites
- Dilapidated institutions and social injustice

These patterns not only erode trust in public systems, but they also leave entire generations trapped in cycles of fear, frustration, and fractured futures.

As one Somali proverb wisely says:

"If you can't resolve your problems in peace, you can't solve war."

The True Cost of Unresolved Conflict

Too often, our pursuit of victory eclipses our commitment to **unity**.

We fight for control while forfeiting our inheritance.

We divide households, communities, and nations, forgetting that the stranger who watches our internal destruction will be the one to **inherit what we were too proud to protect**.

This is the tragedy of many African families. Of many governments. Of many generations.

Where wisdom should have prevailed, **violence** did.

Where collaboration was needed, **competition** reigned.

Where peace was possible, **pride stole the pen** before the agreement could be signed.

When we fail to nurture peace within, we multiply chaos without.

And every war—be it in a household, village, or nation—begins in the heart.

The Path of Moral Imagination

True conflict resolution demands more than negotiation—it calls for **moral imagination**.

It calls for:
- Creativity in the face of stagnation
- Courage in the face of fear
- Collaboration in the face of division

- A willingness to see beyond winning—to seek **healing and wholeness**

We need leadership that does not just change guards through coups or ballots—but leadership that reforms **character**, **culture**, and **conscience**.

Peace is not the absence of tension—it is the **presence of justice**.

Exhortation of the Day

What conflicts have you left to fester in your own relationships, workspaces, or community?

Will you choose to fight for what matters—or fight the very people meant to fight beside you?

Are your disagreements truly worth sacrificing your shared inheritance?

It is time to choose wisdom over ego. Peace over pride. Legacy over temporary power.

Transformative Actions: My Commitment and Contribution

≈ I commit to being a bridge in places of division, a voice of wisdom in moments of tension, and a restorer of peace where conflict threatens purpose.

≈ I will pursue reconciliation not only for personal healing, but for collective restoration.

Now it's your turn:

- Is there a conflict you can resolve today—before the cost becomes irreversible?
- What does it look like to fight for peace in your context?

NOTES
TRANSFORMATIVE ACTIONS: MY COMMITMENT AND CONTRIBUTION

Chapter Thirteen

THE POWER OF FOCUS

Proverb of the Day

"THE HUNTER IN PURSUIT OF AN ELEPHANT DOES NOT STOP TO THROW STONES AT BIRDS."

African Proverb

Reclaiming Africa's Focus

Africa is at a pivotal crossroads—where megatrends collide and the future is being forged in real time.

With a youthful population, rapidly expanding urban centers, and immense economic potential, the continent cannot afford to be distracted. Every second wasted on trivialities is a moment forfeited in the race toward transformation.

The world is shifting—and African cities are becoming more than geographical spaces. They are **epicenters of innovation**, **nuclei of economic activity**, and **incubators of social change**. These urban spaces must be led with **clarity**, **vision**, and **strategic foresight**.

To thrive, African governments, institutions, and leaders must cultivate focus—knowing what truly matters and having the **discipline to prioritize it**.

Focus as a Development Imperative

There is no room for scattered energy when:
- **Infrastructure** is lagging
- **Human capital** remains underdeveloped
- **Policy frameworks** lack alignment with the needs of growing populations

The power of focus lies in its ability to clarify what is urgent and what is essential—and to eliminate what is merely distracting.

A focused leader doesn't confuse movement for momentum.

A focused continent doesn't chase every opportunity—it cultivates what matters most for **long-term flourishing**.

With clear focus:
- Cities are positioned for resilience
- Institutions can design with purpose
- Nations can plan wisely for both now and generations to come

Exhortation of the Day

Focus is a sacred discipline.

When you are called to something greater—when your life has purpose—you cannot afford to stop and throw stones at every criticism, comparison, or distraction.

Some questions do not require answers.

Some noise must be ignored.

Some detours are simply **not your path**.

You were not created to chase birds.

You are in pursuit of **elephants**—of legacy, of transformation, of destiny.

Stay the course.

Transformative Actions: My Commitment and Contribution

≈ I commit to protecting my focus.
≈ To prioritizing what aligns with purpose.
≈ To releasing the need to respond to every voice so I can listen more deeply to the voice that truly matters.
≈ I will pursue my "elephants"—the assignments that stretch beyond me—and refuse to be detained by what is beneath my calling.

Now it's your turn:

- What has been distracting you from your purpose?
- What will you stop chasing—so you can fully pursue the vision that matters most?

NOTES
TRANSFORMATIVE ACTIONS: MY COMMITMENT AND CONTRIBUTION

Chapter Fourteen

Lasting Legacies

Proverb of the Day

"WHERE YOU WILL SIT WHEN YOU ARE OLD SHOWS WHERE YOU STOOD IN YOUTH."

Yoruba Proverb

The Seeds of Legacy

In the face of unrelenting political, social, and economic turbulence, it can be tempting to retreat into passivity—waiting for "the next big thing" to shift our circumstances.

But every day, we are writing the story of our legacy.

Every word spoken, every decision made, every commitment kept or abandoned—we are either building the foundation of something enduring or sleepwalking through life while time quietly moves on.

Africa's youth, in particular, stand at a crossroads. Their stance today will shape the continent's tomorrow.

We cannot afford to be mere observers. We must be **co-creators of the future**.

Rising to the Assignment of Legacy

Each of us has been entrusted with a sacred assignment—a divine call to contribute, to build, to restore.

Legacies are not built in the grand moments alone, but in the ordinary acts of courage, faithfulness, and service.

We must stop waiting for someone else to solve our problems or carry our dreams. Africa's challenges are not just "government problems"—they are **our problems**. And this is **our home**.

We do not get to choose our homeland like we choose a garment. We must instead **honour it** like we honour our ancestors—by planting trees under whose shade we may never sit.

Exhortation of the Day

Where are you standing today?
In complacency or courage?
In entitlement or responsibility?
In memory or movement?
The legacy you leave tomorrow is determined by how you live **today**.
You may not have a title.
You may not hold office.
But you are a leader. In your home, in your street, in your circle.
Rise to that leadership. Walk worthy of your name. Carry your legacy with intention.

Transformative Actions: My Commitment and Contribution

- ≈ I commit to living my legacy with intentionality—knowing that how I live today becomes the inheritance of tomorrow.
- ≈ I will honour the soil that birthed me by sowing seeds of faith, wisdom, justice, and love in every space I occupy.
- ≈ I will not waste time pointing fingers—I will extend hands of action, voice of truth, and heart of service.

Now it's your turn:

- What legacy are you creating today?
- What will future generations say about where you stood—and what you stood for?

NOTES
TRANSFORMATIVE ACTIONS: MY COMMITMENT AND CONTRIBUTION

Chapter Fifteen

BASKING IN PAST GLORY

Proverb of the Day

"MATAKADYA KARE HAANYARADZI MWANA."
(TRANSLATION: YOU CANNOT SILENCE A CRYING AND HUNGRY CHILD WITH MEMORIES OF YESTERDAY'S MEAL.)

Zimbabwean Proverb

Africa's Future Demands Present Action

The once-celebrated "Africa Rising" narrative is being tested. The continent's youthful population—its greatest potential—is facing crises that past triumphs cannot solve.

- Every night, nearly **240 million Africans** go to bed hungry.
- Malnutrition claims the lives of **over half of African children**, many before their fifth birthday.
- Youth unemployment continues to rise, and the looming threat of climate change is displacing millions.

In this storm of pressing realities, we are reminded that **glory stories alone cannot feed the future.**

Africa is young. And it is the young trees that must make up the new forest.

The Danger of Nostalgia Without Innovation

We cannot afford to be lulled into complacency by the successes of yesterday.

While we honour the heroes of the past and celebrate their sacrifices, we must not become **curators of memories** rather than **architects of the future.**

Our inheritance is not simply to recall glory—it is to extend it. To innovate. To lead. To build.

Exhortation of the Day

What solutions are you creating today?
When your name is remembered, will it be for **preserving legacies** or **birthing new ones**?
Africa's future will not rise on nostalgia—it will rise on **present-day conviction** and **courageous action.**

Transformative Actions: My Commitment and Contribution

≈ I commit to honouring the past by building the future.
≈ I will not settle for echoing the exploits of yesterday while neglecting the cries of today.
≈ I choose to rise with clarity, creativity, and courage—to ensure the next generation inherits more than just memories, but living legacies.

Now it's your turn:

- What "meal of the past" are you holding onto?
- What new table will you set to nourish the next generation?

NOTES
TRANSFORMATIVE ACTIONS: MY COMMITMENT AND CONTRIBUTION

Chapter Sixteen

Divide and Rule

Proverb of the Day

"A FIGHT BETWEEN GRASSHOPPERS
IS A JOY TO THE CROW."

Lesotho Proverb

The Destructive Legacy of Divide and Rule

The strategy of **divide and rule**—a tool of colonial power—continues to haunt Africa's political and social landscapes. As defined in the *Advanced Learner's Dictionary*, it is "a method of control by making people disagree and fight among themselves, so they cannot unite to oppose a common oppressor."

What was once imposed by external powers has now become an **internalized method of governance**.

- In many African nations, capable leaders and technocrats are pushed aside by political power plays and factionalism.
- Tribal, ethnic, and ideological divisions are exploited—not healed.
- National unity is sacrificed on the altar of political expediency.

The consequences are dire: stalled economies, social unrest, weakened institutions, and in the worst cases, the slow descent into failed statehood.

From Colonial Tactic to Contemporary Trap

This model of manipulation did not originate in Africa—it was imported during colonial rule to disempower united resistance. Yet its residue remains entrenched in many governance systems today.

Rather than cultivating national vision and collective responsibility, some leaders fuel division for short-term power.

But any government or system built on **division** will eventually crumble. True development only thrives in **trust**, **collaboration**, and **shared vision**.

Exhortation of the Day

Who is benefitting from the divisions we tolerate?
Whether in politics, communities, or families—who stands to gain when we turn against one another?
And more importantly: *what do we lose* when we fail to rise above the fractures?

Transformative Actions: My Commitment and Contribution

≈ I commit to confronting the patterns of division—in myself, in my community, and in the systems I engage with.
≈ I will no longer allow inherited narratives of separation to define our collective future.
≈ I choose to be a bridge, not a barrier. A reconciler, not a rival.

Now it's your turn:

- Where do you see the "divide and rule" mindset operating in your life or society?
- What step can you take to restore unity where division has prevailed?

NOTES
TRANSFORMATIVE ACTIONS: MY COMMITMENT AND CONTRIBUTION

CHAPTER SEVENTEEN

THE POWER
OF THE TONGUE

Proverb of the Day

"THE TONGUE WEIGHS PRACTICALLY NOTHING, BUT SO FEW PEOPLE CAN HOLD IT."

African Proverb

The Invisible Weight of Words

What happens when we release speech into the atmosphere?

We unleash molecules of intention that ripple through time and space—shaping atmospheres, bending realities, building legacies…

or tearing them down.

Africa suffers not for lack of voices, but for lack of **disciplined, intelligent, and visionary speech**.

There is too much talk and too little transformative implementation.

The result?

A deficit in trans-generational planning, fractured families, weak alignment between words and actions, and a continent groaning beneath the weight of promises unfulfilled.

The Village Madman and the Sacredness of Speech

Growing up in the rural farming lands of Chivhu, I vividly remember how our elders hushed us—especially as we ventured through thick forests to gather firewood or crossed rivers at dusk.

We were constantly reminded: "Don't talk too much in the bush."

There were unseen powers, they warned—mystical forces in the trees and shadows that could steal your words, silence your voice, or twist your tongue forever.

At the time, we didn't understand. We were children—full of chatter, giggles, and curiosity. But the harsh *pull-and-twist ear pinches* we received when we disobeyed made the lesson unforgettable.

My cousin and I would feel the *heat of that discipline* lingering long after the moment had passed, serving as a burning reminder that some silences are sacred.

Later at home, we were told the story of Boreman, the village madman.

They said he once dared to insult the unseen during a drunken rant as he staggered home from the beerhall.

He had laughed loudly and mocked the spirits, claiming they had no power over him.

From that night, he was never the same.

He roamed barefoot through the village—wild-eyed, muttering nonsense, disconnected from time and space.

Some said his tongue had been cursed. Others said his mind had been stolen.

To us, **Boreman was more than a madman—he was a living proverb.**

A reminder that **speech is sacred**, and every word released has an assignment in the spiritual realm.

Wholesome Speech: A Leadership Virtue

Wholesome speech flows from a transformed mind. It is:

- **Considerate**
- **Purposeful**
- **Life-giving**

Wholesome speech restores dignity, rebuilds trust, and reinforces peace.

Unwholesome speech—rooted in bitterness, careless emotion, or ignorance—can destroy what generations have laboured to build.

We've seen this across the African continent:

conflicts ignited by divisive rhetoric,

communities torn apart by tribal slurs,

nations destabilized by **the sharp, reckless tongues of the powerful.**

Words are not just spoken. **They are sown.**

A Call to Speak with Intention

Your tongue may be light in weight,

but its impact is **immeasurable**.

Before you speak, ask yourself:

- Does this build or break?
- Does it heal or harm?
- Is this speech aligned with the future I want to see?

You are not just speaking into the air.

You are sowing into the unseen.

And the harvest will reflect what your words have planted.

Transformative Actions: My Commitment and Contribution

≈ I commit to being a **guardian of my words**.

≈ I will speak with **clarity, compassion, and conviction**.

≈ I will use my voice to build **homes, not haunt them—nations, not ruins.**

≈ I recognize that my speech carries **creative power**.

≈ With that awareness, I choose to release words that **bless, uplift, and transform**.

Now it's your turn:

- What patterns of speech do you need to unlearn or release?
- How will you begin to speak in a way that **honours your future** and **shapes Africa's destiny**?

NOTES
TRANSFORMATIVE ACTIONS: MY COMMITMENT AND CONTRIBUTION

Chapter Eighteen

What Do You Answer To?

Proverb of the Day

"IT IS NOT WHAT YOU ARE CALLED BUT WHAT YOU ANSWER TO THAT MATTERS."

African Proverb

When Identity Is Under Siege

Inferiority complex has become a silent epidemic across African nations.

From the market stalls to executive boardrooms, a dangerous belief persists:

foreign is superior, local is suspect.

This mindset is not just external—it is deeply internal.

It distorts how we see ourselves, how we value our work, and how we treat one another.

It causes us to **whisper apologies for being African**,

to **underrate our produce**,

to **underprice our worth**,

and to **undervalue our power**.

It's not just about what the world calls us.

The deeper question is: **what do we respond to?**

The Colonized Mindset: The Enemy Within

From childhood, we've heard phrases like:

"Don't behave like someone with a slave mind."

Yet, these words were often spoken lightly—like a bad mood that would pass.

But the truth is sobering.

The colonial mindset is **not a fleeting illness**—

it is a **virulent condition** that has infected generations.

It's the voice that whispers, *"Your best will never be good enough."*

It's the internalized oppression that tells us to tear down one another,

to **mimic the oppressor**,

to fight over crumbs while forgetting we own the harvest.

Bobby E. Wright once observed:

"We have never been trained to kill Europeans. But we seem able to kill each other instinctively."

This mindset breeds self-hate, glorifies imported values, and numbs us to injustice—especially when we are the ones inflicting it.

Mental Liberation Begins at Home

Carter G. Woodson warned us:

"When you control a man's thinking, you do not have to worry about his actions. He will find his 'proper place' and stay in it."

We need to start *replacing the labels* we have responded to with *new declarations*.

And the most logical starting point is the home.

- Let us train our children to answer to **greatness**, not inferiority.
- To see their melanin, names, languages, and origins as **assets**, not accidents.
- To recognize Africa not as a deficit, but as **a divine assignment**.

Early childhood—especially ages 0–11—is where seeds of liberation or limitation are planted.

If we wait until adulthood, we may be too late.

Let us build culturally affirming curricula, nurturing nurseries, and homes where Afrocentric values are not imposed, but *incubated*.

We must speak openly about historical trauma, **post-colonial stress**, and **the effects of internalized oppression**—then boldly walk the path of healing, restoration, and renewal.

Transformative Actions: My Commitment and Contribution

≈ I commit to **breaking internal chains** that disguise themselves as humility or realism.
≈ I will **answer only to the truth** of who I am:
≈ Created with purpose.

≈ Rooted in legacy.
≈ Called for more.
≈ I will nurture Afrocentric identity in my home, community, and platform—and honour the power of names, narratives, and Nationhood.

Now it's your turn:

- What have you been called that no longer deserves your response?
- What will you begin answering to—starting today?

NOTES
TRANSFORMATIVE ACTIONS: MY COMMITMENT AND CONTRIBUTION

CHAPTER NINETEEN

STRATEGIC THINKING

Proverb of the Day

"IF YOU WISH TO MOVE MOUNTAINS TOMORROW,
YOU MUST START BY LIFTING STONES TODAY."

African Proverb

From Survival to Significance

Life moves between three paradigms: **Survival**, **Success**, and **Significance**.

The decisions we make—daily and deliberately—determine which door we open, which corridors we navigate, and how deeply we experience fulfillment.

Yet, in a world fixated on urgency and short-term wins, **strategic thinking** is often postponed, dismissed, or overlooked.

But destiny cannot be downloaded.

Vision must be stewarded with intention, and tomorrow's triumphs must be seeded in today's sacrifices.

Africa's Future Demands Strategic Visionaries

As Africa rises to claim her rightful place in the global narrative, we are called not just to dream—but to **design**.

Not just to survive—but to **strategize**.

In 2013, the African Union introduced **Agenda 2063**, a bold and visionary roadmap to shape the continent's future over 50 years.

But vision without implementation is a mirage.

Too many development frameworks have failed—not for lack of hope—but for lack of capacity, coherence, and committed follow-through.

To realize transformation, we must:
- Advocate for policy alignment and public awareness
- Build institutions that can monitor, evaluate, and adapt
- Involve think tanks and thought leaders as critical actors in shaping reform and progress
- Elevate strategic foresight as a national asset—not a luxury

Africa cannot afford to outsource its future.

The time for intentional, evidence-based, and values-driven planning is now.

Lifting the Stones Today

From war to weak governance, from poverty to unfair trade systems—Africa's mountains are not immovable.

But they won't shift through wishful thinking.

We need game-changing leaders who:
- See beneath the surface
- Think long-term
- Act with both urgency and wisdom
- Lead with bold humility

We must move from **reactivity to strategy**, from **firefighting to future-building**.

Transformative Actions: My Commitment and Contribution

≈ I commit to cultivating a strategic mind—one that doesn't simply chase outcomes, but designs systems.
≈ I will embrace thoughtful planning and courageous implementation.
≈ Africa deserves more than temporary fixes—it deserves lasting frameworks.
≈ I will invest my energy not only in vision casting, but in capacity building—lifting the stones of reform, equity, and innovation today.

Now it's your turn:

- What "stones" do you need to lift today to prepare for the future you desire?
- How are you embedding strategic thinking into your daily decisions—personal, professional, and communal?

NOTES
TRANSFORMATIVE ACTIONS: MY COMMITMENT AND CONTRIBUTION

CHAPTER TWENTY

THE POWER OF VULNERABILITY

Proverb of the Day

"MBUDZI KUZVARIRA PAVANHU KUDA KUTANDIRWA IMBWA."

TRANSLATION: A GOAT GIVES BIRTH IN PUBLIC HOPING TO FIND SOMEONE TO CHASE AWAY THE DOGS.

Zimbabwean Proverb

Embracing the Courage to Be Seen

As human beings, we carry within us not just strengths and victories, but fears, flaws, and fragile spaces. And yet, in a world that glorifies perfection, vulnerability is often mistaken for weakness.

We are conditioned to hide our pain, polish our imperfections, and power through our brokenness. But in doing so, we trade authenticity for acceptance—and connection for performance.

Vulnerability is not the absence of strength—it is the evidence of courage.

It is the willingness to be seen in our wholeness—both the wounds and the wisdom.

The Paradox of Power

True power is not found in masks, but in meaning.

Not in posturing, but in presence.

When we admit our fears, name our needs, and share our struggles, we create space for healing and deeper connection. Vulnerability:

- Builds trust and transparency in relationships
- Deepens empathy and emotional intelligence

- Creates safe spaces for truth-telling and reconciliation
- Allows communities and nations to ask for help without shame

We are not diminished by expressing pain—we are *expanded*.

A Cultural and Communal Reflection

In African contexts, moments of public vulnerability—like the metaphor in today's proverb—are not about shame, but survival.

When the goat gives birth in front of others, it is not seeking attention—it is crying for protection.

So too, individuals, families, and nations sometimes expose their pain in public spaces—not for pity, but for partnership.

The real test of character is not how we present ourselves in strength, but how we respond to the weakness of others.

Do we mock?
Do we protect?
Or do we walk away?

A Boomerang of Compassion or Condemnation

What we do when someone is at their lowest says more about us than it does about them. Life has a strange boomerang effect—the compassion or cruelty we sow in others' vulnerable moments will one day circle back to us.

We must remember:
- Every soul has its breaking point
- Every leader will have a valley season
- Every nation may one day cry out for mercy

Let us lead, relate, and rebuild from a place of tenderness and truth.

Transformative Actions: My Commitment and Contribution

≈ I choose vulnerability as a path to connection.
≈ I will lead with openness, hold space for others, and meet brokenness with compassion.
≈ In my family, work, and community—I will not weaponize weakness. I will honor it.

Now it's your turn:

- How have you viewed vulnerability in your life—as a weakness or a window?
- When others reveal their struggles, how do you respond?
- What would it look like to embrace vulnerability as a leadership virtue in your home, organization, or nation?

NOTES
TRANSFORMATIVE ACTIONS: MY COMMITMENT AND CONTRIBUTION

CHAPTER TWENTY-ONE

HIGH SEAT VERSUS LOW SEAT ISSUES

Proverb of the Day

"KAMOTO KAMBEREVERE KAKAPISA MATANDA MBERI."

(TRANSLATION: A SMALL FIRE LEFT UNATTENDED CAN BURN THE BIG LOGS AHEAD.)

Zimbabwean Proverb

Conversations That Will Shape Africa: Asking the Right Questions

In *Discover The Gift*, Mary Manin Morrissey teaches:

"The quality of life is determined by the quality of the questions we learn to ask."

Questions, she says, are the access point to the mind that holds the answers we seek.

Africa is a continent brimming with dialogue—conferences, summits, and official gatherings fill the calendars of those seated at the top. Lavish delegations are sent to represent us at prestigious global events. Grand resolutions are made. Yet, the outcomes of these engagements often fail to trickle down and touch the lives of those they are meant to serve.

Could it be that we are prioritizing the wrong things?

Are we asking the right questions at the wrong tables?

Are we focusing on *"low seat"* issues while seated at *"high seats"* of influence and authority?

When Leadership Misses the Mark

The term *"high seat issues"* symbolizes the weighty, strategic matters that affect entire systems, institutions, and generations.

"Low seat issues," on the other hand, may refer to short-sighted, individualistic concerns that are urgent but not always important—decisions that appear significant in the moment but lack lasting impact.

When those in positions of power become consumed with ego-driven optics, petty rivalries, personal gains, and superficial agendas, the real work suffers.

And when seemingly small issues are ignored—those *"low seat"* matters left unattended—they can spiral into national headaches that drain resources and disorient focus.

A Continent at a Crossroads

Einstein once said,

"If I had 60 minutes to solve a problem and my life depended on it, I'd spend 55 minutes determining the right question to ask."

The truth is: Africa's future depends not just on action, but on **aligned priorities**.

We cannot afford to be distracted by noise, appearances, or unnecessary bureaucracy.

We must evaluate every conversation by asking:
- *Is this building a better tomorrow?*
- *Is this aligned with the people's cry?*
- *Does this advance Africa's healing, dignity, and growth?*

The current model—where "big chefs" travel across continents to engage in abstract dialogues that yield no tangible benefit for citizens—is unsustainable. We are hemorrhaging time, resources, and trust.

Exhortation: We Must Ask Better Questions

As leaders, thinkers, and citizens—we are called to steward the issues that truly matter.

We must rise above distractions and low-level debates.

We must not only sit at high tables—but bring high-value thinking, long-term vision, and people-centered priorities with us.

And we must never forget that the smallest spark, if ignored, can raze the whole forest.

Transformative Actions: My Commitment and Contribution

≈ I commit to prioritizing what matters most.
≈ I will discern between noise and necessity, between the optics of influence and the substance of service.
≈ I will be intentional in asking—and listening to—the right questions.
≈ Africa deserves leadership that is focused, courageous, and deeply accountable.

Now it's your turn:

- What "low seat" distractions are drawing you away from the higher purpose of your role or calling?
- How can you begin to redirect your energy toward high-impact, generational solutions?

NOTES
TRANSFORMATIVE ACTIONS: MY COMMITMENT AND CONTRIBUTION

Chapter Twenty-Two

SO RICH YET SO POOR

Proverb of the Day

"THE WEALTH WHICH ENSLAVES THE OWNER ISN'T WEALTH."

African Proverb

The Wealth-Poverty Paradox in Africa

Why is Africa—the cradle of mankind, the second largest and second most populous continent on the planet, endowed with staggering natural and mineral wealth—also home to some of the world's poorest populations?

Who or what is responsible for this painful contradiction?

Are the colonialists solely to blame, or have we as Africans contributed to our own economic captivity?

And more importantly—**can this conundrum be solved?** Or are we doomed to repeat decades of deprivation, underdevelopment, and dependence?

Africa: The Richest Poor Man on Earth

It almost defies logic—an unimaginably wealthy land reduced to a beggar's bowl. A continent holding the keys to global prosperity, yet locked in cycles of poverty, disease, and instability. The numbers don't lie: Africa houses the majority of the world's strategic resources, yet remains the most impoverished continent.

How does this happen?

It's as if we're watching the richest poor man in the world struggle to survive while the world thrives off his inheritance.

Extractive Industries and Economic Extraction

As Baffour Ankomah, a Ghanaian journalist and editor powerfully puts it:

"The great sinners in this massive rip-off have been companies in the extractive sector... with the help of the political and economic muscle of their home countries, they browbeat African governments to sign away mining concessions that ensure that Africans get very little for their God-given resources."

But we cannot solely blame outsiders.

Yes, colonial legacies persist. But Africa's enduring poverty amidst wealth is also the result of internal fractures—**corruption, conflict, compromised governance, and a deficit of courageous, integrity-driven leadership.**

We do not suffer from a lack of resources.

We suffer from a lack of stewardship.

A Call for Transformational Integrity

Africa has no shortage of intellect. Our leaders are highly educated, internationally trained, and globally respected. Yet, leadership in many contexts has failed to translate knowledge into justice, potential into productivity, and wealth into wellbeing.

The future of Africa will not be determined by how much gold lies beneath her soil, but by the values that lie within her people.

Transformative Actions: My Commitment and Contribution

≈ I commit to challenging systems that exploit Africa's wealth while keeping her people poor.
≈ I choose to embody integrity, advocate for transparency, and steward influence with wisdom and humility.
≈ I will raise my voice for economic justice—and lend my hands to ethical leadership.

Now it's your turn:

- What role are you playing in the story of Africa's wealth?
- Are you guarding it—or giving it away?
- Will future generations call you a custodian of legacy—or a bystander to loss?

NOTES
TRANSFORMATIVE ACTIONS: MY COMMITMENT AND CONTRIBUTION

CHAPTER TWENTY-THREE

MAKING A DIFFERENCE

Proverb of the Day

"IF YOU THINK YOU ARE TOO SMALL TO MAKE A DIFFERENCE, YOU HAVEN'T SPENT A NIGHT WITH A MOSQUITO."

African Proverb

Every Action Matters

While governments and officials have their part to play, the restoration of Africa's dignity cannot be outsourced. True change will only come when each individual applies themselves with conviction, integrity, and purpose—right where they are.

Whether in a boardroom, a classroom, a garden, or a parliament, making a difference does not begin with status or wealth. It begins with willingness.

The Lazy Townspeople

A traditional story retold by Kate Awo Fumey

Once upon a time, there was a town where the people were exceedingly lazy. They didn't like to do any work—yards overgrew with weeds, streets remained filthy, and no one tended their vegetable patches. The place was a disgrace.

Every so often, the chief would try to launch a cleanup campaign. But only a handful would show up, and even they would stop after a day or two. The weeds always won.

One day, a fierce hurricane blew through the town. Among the damage, a massive tree was hurled across the main road leading to the marketplace. Traders came, saw the obstruction, and simply walked around it. "I don't have time to move it—I must get to market," they said.

Days passed. The tree remained. The chief, tired of excuses, devised a plan. Before dawn, he and his servants buried a stash of gold beneath the tree, then summoned all the townspeople later that afternoon.

"Let's work together," he urged them. "If we all help, we can move this tree quickly."

But complaints filled the air:

"The hurricane put it there. Let the hurricane remove it."

"Why bother? We can walk around it."

"What's the rush?"

Just as the chief was about to give up, a poor, skinny young farmer—without family or reputation—stepped forward.

"I'll try," he said.

He strained and struggled while the crowd mocked and murmured. No one helped—except the chief's servants, who were finally instructed to assist. Together, they rolled the tree away.

The chief then led the young farmer to the hidden spot beneath the road and asked him to dig. To the shock of all, the farmer unearthed a stash of gold.

"This gold is yours," the chief declared. "You earned it through your willingness and action."

Then turning to the lazy crowd, he said:

"Let this be a lesson. Laziness reaps nothing. But those who rise and work—even alone—will always find reward."

Exhortation of the Day

Sons and daughters of Africa—
You don't have to be many. You don't have to be loud.
But you **must** be willing.
Willing to step forward.
Willing to push while others watch.
Willing to believe that your effort matters.
You are not too small to make a difference.

Transformative Actions: My Commitment and Contribution

- ≈ I commit to showing up, even when others don't.
- ≈ I will press forward, even if I must go alone.
- ≈ I believe my obedience to act may unlock generational blessings— hidden treasures that only courage can uncover.

Now it's your turn:

- What is the "tree" blocking the road in your community or calling?
- Are you waiting for others to move first—or will you be the one who tries?

NOTES
TRANSFORMATIVE ACTIONS: MY COMMITMENT AND CONTRIBUTION

Chapter Twenty-Four

Wisdom in Counsel

Proverb of the Day

"ADVICE IS A STRANGER; IF HE'S WELCOME HE STAYS FOR THE NIGHT; IF NOT, HE LEAVES THE SAME DAY."

Malagasy Proverb

An Ancient Tradition in Urgent Times

Across the great villages and kingdoms of Africa, counsel was never random noise—it was sacred.

Elders held space for truth.

The young were expected to listen.

And in the quiet fireside hours, destinies were shaped through simple, solemn words.

Today, on the youngest continent, with 65% of Africans under the age of 35, this ancient practice of mentorship must not fade. If anything, it must be revived, formalized, and wielded with urgency.

Africa cannot afford to squander the strength of her youth nor the wisdom of her elders.

One without the other is a broken bridge.

But together—they are the path to rebirth.

Reforming Africa Through Counsel and Succession

The often-repeated truth that *Africa's problem is not resources, but leadership* has echoed across platforms for decades.

But what is leadership without succession?

What is succession without mentorship?

And what is mentorship without values?

Africa's reformation must be grounded in values-based leadership and **deliberate, strategic mentorship**—not the casual handover of titles, but the intentional impartation of wisdom, integrity, and responsibility.

The Ethiopian proverb reminds us:

"If you refuse an elder's advice, you will walk the whole day."

The walk becomes even longer when generations fail to build continuity, losing precious momentum with every gap in guidance.

Biblical Blueprints, African Futures

From Moses and Joshua, Elijah and Elisha, to Paul and Timothy—the Bible is rich with examples of mentorship that led to legacy.

Not just spiritual legacies, but systems-shifting leadership.

Africa must cultivate such models.

Let leaders rise who understand the sacred weight of stewardship, the quiet strength of servant-leadership, and the discipline of foresight.

Let new voices emerge—rooted in heritage, fluent in innovation, and bold enough to hold power with humility.

A New Breed Must Rise

The Africa we long for will not be willed into existence by inspiration alone.

It must be *built*—stone by stone, generation by generation, leader by leader.

Let us raise a critical mass of new leaders with:
- **Integrity that does not falter when no one is watching.**
- **Confidence that is not arrogance, but assurance of purpose.**
- **An abundance mindset that seeks collective elevation.**
- **Excellence that refuses mediocrity in policy, service, or personal conduct.**

The future is not a mystery.
It is a mission.

Transformative Actions: My Commitment and Contribution

≈ I commit to honouring counsel—both giving and receiving it with humility and grace.
≈ I will be intentional in mentoring others and in seeking wisdom from those who've gone before me.
≈ I will work to build systems that do not just celebrate good leadership—but sustain it across generations.

Now it's your turn:

- Who are your mentors?
- Who are you mentoring?
- What kind of legacy are you preparing to pass on?

NOTES
TRANSFORMATIVE ACTIONS: MY COMMITMENT AND CONTRIBUTION

CHAPTER TWENTY-FIVE

LOVE, STABILITY
AND PANDEMICS

Proverb of the Day

"WHAT YOU HELP A CHILD TO LOVE CAN BE MORE IMPORTANT THAN WHAT YOU HELP HIM TO LEARN."

African Proverb

Hidden Epidemics and Healing Foundations

When we talk about Africa's underdevelopment, we often begin with the usual suspects—colonial legacies, economic isolation, or political dysfunction. But there's another, often overlooked thread silently pulling at the fabric of progress: *infectious diseases*.

Long before COVID-19 made the world pause, Africa had already been battling waves of pandemics—from HIV/AIDS to malaria, cholera to Ebola. These are not just health crises; they are development disruptors. They steal time, energy, and resources from already struggling systems. They orphan children, destabilize economies, and deepen poverty.

Worldwide, one-fourth of all deaths are caused by infectious diseases. In Africa, the percentage is even higher. If we are to rise, we must not only fight these diseases—we must *transform how we respond* to them.

Conversations on a Continental Response

Michel Sidibé, the former Executive Director of UNAIDS, once declared that Africa must craft **its own vision** for responding to pandemics. His call is more urgent now than ever before.

Here are five critical shifts he proposed—still painfully relevant today:

1. **Resource Management**
   Prioritize wisely. Allocate strategically. Preserve domestic funding for health—don't depend solely on donor aid.
2. **Human Capacity**
   Train the right people in the right numbers and *pay them fairly*. If our health systems fail the people who sustain them, they cannot survive a crisis.
3. **Research and Regulation**
   Invest in research that solves our problems. Harmonize our pharmaceutical and clinical systems to eliminate waste and duplication.
4. **Trade and Access**
   Make access to medicine a permanent right, not a privilege. Too many still die because life-saving drugs are locked behind policy or profit.
5. **Mutual Accountability**
   Real change cannot happen to people—it must happen with them. Civil society, communities, and families must all be engaged.

"Without mutual accountability, we cannot convince our own Ministers of Finance, donor agencies, or even our neighbours that Africa's health is worth investing in."
— Michel Sidibé

The Role of the African Family

Beyond systems and funding mechanisms lies a more foundational sphere of transformation: *the family*.

Pandemics don't just expose weak healthcare systems—they reveal the deeper fractures in how we love, relate, and build intimacy. That's why any meaningful response must go beyond clinics and policies to reach *homes and hearts*.

In Zimbabwe, a Shona proverb wisely says:

"Zingizi gonyera pamwe, maruva enyika haaperi."
(Settle down with one woman; there will always be beautiful women in the world.)

Another African pearl reminds us:

"A happy man marries the girl he loves, but a happier man loves the girl he marries."

These are not just quaint sayings—they are blueprints for love, stability, and responsibility.

When we pass these values to our children—not only through lectures, but through lived example—we equip them to resist risky behaviours, navigate peer pressures, and build families that are resilient, not reckless.

Transformative Actions: My Commitment and Contribution

≈ I commit to honouring and sharing values of faithfulness, emotional wisdom, and responsible relationships.
≈ I will advocate for systems that protect health but also nurture *wholeness*.

≈ I believe pandemics are not just biological—they are spiritual, social, and cultural. Healing must touch every layer.

Now it's your turn:

- What values are you modelling for those watching you?
- How are you strengthening your family, your community, and your continent through the power of love and stability?

NOTES
TRANSFORMATIVE ACTIONS: MY COMMITMENT AND CONTRIBUTION

CHAPTER TWENTY-SIX

THINKING BEFORE YOU ACT

Proverb of the Day

"WAKURUMIDZA KUMEDZA, KUTSENGA UCHADA."
(TRANSLATION: YOU SWALLOWED TOO QUICKLY—
YOU'LL STILL NEED TO CHEW.)

Zimbabwean Proverb

Freedom, Spontaneity, and the Illusion of Liberty

"Live for the moment!"

"Be spontaneous!"

"Act like today is your last!"

Such mantras echo in our modern world, disguised as freedom and packaged as joy. The advertising industry has mastered this message, calling us to drop everything for adventure, to choose pleasure over prudence, and to treat caution as a hindrance to authenticity.

But beneath the glitter of spontaneity lies a more sobering truth: *impulsiveness without reflection can be destructive.*

Spontaneity has its place—but it must be tethered to wisdom.

When we act without regard for consequence, without awareness of timing or context, we risk hurting others and sabotaging our own futures.

Yes, there is beauty in being fully present. But there is also *danger* in mistaking the present moment as permission to abandon purpose.

The Trap of the Unexamined Impulse

True freedom is not the ability to do whatever we want, whenever we feel like it.

True freedom, as philosophers like Jean-Paul Sartre observed, carries responsibility.

If spontaneity becomes a license to escape the weight of decision, we may find ourselves prisoners of regret—ensnared not by what was done to us, but by what we did without thinking.

The dream of absolute liberty is appealing in a world saturated with schedules and performance pressures.

Yet freedom *without foresight* becomes recklessness.

It's one thing to break routine with joyful spontaneity; it's another to abandon wise restraint in the name of "just being free."

The Quiet Power of Deliberate Choices

Every choice we make involves *costs and benefits*.

Often, we rush toward the reward without counting the cost.

But lasting success—whether in leadership, relationships, or personal growth—comes from cultivating *decision-making as a discipline*.

Ask yourself:
- What am I really trying to achieve?
- What will this action cost me—and those around me?
- What long-term impact could this have?

Sometimes the most courageous thing we can do is *pause*.
To chew before we swallow.
To reflect before we speak.
To sit with a feeling before acting on it.

Exhortation of the Day

≈ The next time you feel an impulse—whether to act, to respond, or to speak—*pause and ponder.*

≈ Ask: Is this worth the price it might demand?

≈ That single moment of thought could save you years of pain, loss, or regret.

≈ Let your life be governed by *intentional wisdom*, not fleeting whims.

Transformative Actions: My Commitment and Contribution

≈ I commit to pausing before I proceed.

≈ To asking questions that matter before making decisions that last.

≈ I will be thoughtful with my speech, strategic in my steps, and accountable for my actions.

≈ I embrace spontaneity as a gift—but I will not let it dethrone wisdom.

Now it's your turn:

- Where in your life are you acting without reflection?
- What one decision today needs a little more time, prayer, or counsel before you move?

NOTES
TRANSFORMATIVE ACTIONS: MY COMMITMENT AND CONTRIBUTION

CHAPTER TWENTY-SEVEN

THE POWER OF COMMUNITY

Proverb of the Day

"STICKS IN A BUNDLE ARE UNBREAKABLE."

African Proverb

The Strength of Togetherness

Africa's reformation will not come from the top alone—it will emerge when both leaders and grassroots communities take ownership of their development journeys.

This calls for a renewed commitment to values-based leadership, decentralized governance, and the restoration of ethical systems.

It begins with one person. One village. One dream that's shared and pursued collectively.

We must challenge mindsets and equip sons and daughters of the continent to self-introspect, design, and implement contextual solutions in their own fields—because community is not just where we live, it's where transformation takes root.

Success Stories from Mali: A Model of Community-Led Empowerment

Tostan's Community Empowerment Program (CEP) offers a shining example of what is possible when development is community-driven and values-centered.

This three-year program equips communities with human rights education, literacy, project management, and health tools—anchored by **Community Management Committees (CMCs)**, where half the members are women.

Let's explore the multi-dimensional impact this has had in **Mali**:

Education

In **Kalkoun**, the CMC rebuilt six classrooms and constructed a latrine—drastically increasing school attendance, especially for girls.

In **Tama** and **Beleninko**, communities led similar initiatives to ensure children have dignified, functional learning environments.

Health

In **Hamaribougou**, seasonal flooding once cut off access to clinics. The local CMC partnered with nearby health centers to stock emergency supplies and purchased medication using community funds.

In one quarter alone:
- 525 prenatal consultations
- 124 safe births
- 399 postnatal visits
- 8,621 children vaccinated

Health improved—because the *community* took responsibility.

Child Protection

In **Zana**, symbolic sanctions were introduced for parents who neglected basic care (e.g., not providing shoes).

CMCs also led campaigns to **end child marriage and female genital cutting**, working alongside elders and faith leaders to reinforce human rights values.

Environment

Communities conducted **494 clean-up campaigns**, built **325 improved stoves**, and planted **1,800 trees** across multiple villages—fueling environmental restoration from the ground up.

Economic Growth

Community-managed **microfinance funds** enabled women like **Douguô Coulibaly** to grow onion-selling businesses, increasing their incomes and influence.

In just four months:
- 480 loans were disbursed
- All loans were repaid in full
- A second cycle of 480 new recipients (370 women) was launched

This is not charity. It's **sustainable prosperity**, driven by trust, accountability, and shared growth.

The Call for Communal Consciousness

Africa doesn't need imported blueprints—it needs **empowered communities**, equipped with knowledge, integrity, and unity.

When ordinary people come together for extraordinary purpose, mountains move.

Transformative Actions: My Commitment and Contribution

≈ I commit to championing community-led solutions.
≈ I will not wait for change to come from above—I will plant seeds of transformation in my own backyard.
≈ I will honour the power of unity and invest in building safe, vibrant, and visionary communities.

Now it's your turn:

- What strength lies untapped in your own community?
- How can you rally others to pursue collective development today?

NOTES
TRANSFORMATIVE ACTIONS: MY COMMITMENT AND CONTRIBUTION

Chapter Twenty-Eight

DYSFUNCTIONS FROM OVER-DEPENDENCY

Proverb of the Day

"MOMBE YEKURUNZIRWA NDEYEKUKAMA
WAKARINDE NZIRA."

(TRANSLATION: YOU CAN NEVER USE BORROWED THINGS WITH
THE FREEDOM YOU WOULD HAVE IF IT WAS YOURS.)

Zimbabwean Proverb

Developing Alternatives to Financial Aid

For too long, Africa has been held hostage by the illusion of help. The cycle of dependency—though often clothed in diplomatic jargon and aid agreements—has silently weakened the continent's self-reliance and capacity for innovation.

We must boldly state the truth: **Africa does not lack resources—it suffers from the dysfunctions bred by over-dependency**. A continent so rich in minerals, intellect, and youth potential should not be trapped in a web of economic stagnation because of aid structures that often rob more than they restore.

Despite receiving billions in aid annually, Africa continues to experience **capital flight**—with far more money flowing out of the continent in the form of loan interest repayments, resource exploitation, and corporate tax avoidance than ever flows in. It is this **economic paradox** that leaves many African nations unable to meet even the most basic social needs of their people.

Beyond Dependency: A Call for Resourceful Leadership

If Africa is to rise, its leaders must begin to **think beyond aid** and craft strategic policies that challenge the status quo. This includes:

- **Rejecting policies** that disempower indigenous initiatives.
- **Negotiating trade deals and partnerships** that respect Africa's autonomy.
- **Building alternatives**—not only in financing, but in energy, education, technology, and innovation.
- **Investing in homegrown solutions** such as solar power, wind energy, and desert agriculture—using the sun-soaked plains, the vast windswept deserts, and the ingenuity of Africa's people.

This is not merely a matter of economics—it is a **reclamation of dignity**.

Leadership That Liberates

This shift demands a new breed of leadership—leaders who are not afraid of rivalry, not obsessed with short-term political gain, but focused on trans-generational transformation. True visionaries will rise above fear, tribalism, and self-preservation, and instead unite around a **continental agenda** for prosperity, innovation, and justice.

Africa's rebirth will not come from borrowed systems or external validation. It will be sparked by courageous decisions, cultivated through deliberate investments in local capacity, and sustained by **a people who believe in their own power to thrive**.

Transformative Actions: My Commitment and Contribution

≈ I commit to thinking beyond dependency and championing innovation.
≈ I will use my voice and platform to advocate for self-reliance and integrity in leadership.
≈ I choose to believe in Africa's capacity to rise—not through borrowed strength, but through the unlocking of her own wealth.

Now it's your turn:

- What inherited dependency patterns do you need to unlearn?
- How will you contribute to building an Africa that stands on its own feet?

NOTES
TRANSFORMATIVE ACTIONS: MY COMMITMENT AND CONTRIBUTION

CHAPTER TWENTY-NINE

THE CANCER
OF CORRUPTION

Proverb of the Day

"STEALING A DRUM IS EASY, BUT FINDING A PLACE TO BEAT IT IS NOT."

Nigerian Proverb

The Hidden Costs of Corruption

Corruption is more than a moral failure—it is an entrenched system of self-enrichment that eats away at a nation's potential like a malignant cancer. It siphons off resources meant for the common good and diverts them into the pockets of a few, leaving citizens to languish in underdevelopment and poverty.

Despite Africa's abundant natural wealth—oil, gold, diamonds, fertile land—**many nations remain trapped at the bottom of the United Nations Development Index**, not because of resource scarcity, but because of internal sabotage.

Corruption is not only about bribes exchanged under the table. It is **about poor governance, warped priorities, opaque decision-making, and the institutionalisation of greed**. The consequences are catastrophic:

- Roads that wash away with the first rain.
- Hospitals without medicines or trained staff.
- Schools built on paper but never in real life.
- Loans acquired in the name of national development, but ending up in offshore accounts.

And tragically, **it is the poor who suffer the most**.

When Greed Becomes Governance

The true tragedy of corruption lies in what it replaces:
- **Vision is replaced by personal ambition.**
- **Service is replaced by self-interest.**
- **Hope is replaced by helplessness.**

Corruption diverts public funds from life-saving programs and squanders them on vanity projects or white elephants that serve no one but those who signed the deals. It widens the gap between rich and poor, weakens social trust, and often sparks conflict when disenfranchised groups rise in protest.

In some countries, **drugs meant for rural clinics can be found on the shelves of private pharmacies.** Public officers accept bribes to approve substandard roads, buildings, and infrastructure that later collapse, sometimes with deadly consequences.

When governments ignore national priorities in favour of projects that yield personal profit, **development becomes a façade**, and the nation's debt burden grows while its people's dignity shrinks.

Restoring Integrity: Principles of Good Governance

To cure this cancer, Africa must rise on the pillars of **good governance**, where integrity is the default, not the exception.

Some of the most critical principles include:
- **Honesty**—Integrity and moral uprightness must define leadership at every level.
- **Transparency**—Processes must be open, clear, and available to the people.
- **Responsiveness**—Concerns of citizens must be heard and addressed promptly.
- **Accountability**—All who hold public office must answer to the people and the law.

- **Rule of Law**—No one is above the law. Impartial enforcement is non-negotiable.
- **Efficiency and Effectiveness**—Every resource must be used wisely, with measurable impact.
- **Fairness**—Policies must be inclusive and just, benefitting all, not just the privileged few.
- **Separation of Powers**—Independent systems prevent conflicts of interest and abuse.
- **Justice**—There must be moral clarity and the courage to protect the vulnerable.

Transformative Actions: My Commitment and Contribution

≈ I commit to resisting corruption in all its forms.
≈ I will uphold integrity, speak truth to power, and promote transparency in every sphere I influence.
≈ I will be part of the solution—advocating for justice, fairness, and accountability in my community and beyond.

Now it's your turn:

- In what ways have you witnessed corruption erode your community or nation?
- What personal commitment will you make to uphold integrity and justice?

NOTES
TRANSFORMATIVE ACTIONS: MY COMMITMENT AND CONTRIBUTION

Chapter Thirty

GREED AND SELFISHNESS

Proverb of the Day

"DON'T TAKE ANOTHER MOUTHFUL BEFORE YOU HAVE SWALLOWED WHAT IS IN YOUR MOUTH."

Malagasy Proverb

The Appetite That Never Satisfies

Greed is a hungry fire—it consumes, devours, and always asks for more.

It is a root cause of inequality, corruption, political instability, and fractured communities across the African continent. Where selfishness abounds, Ubuntu dies.

Africa is not poor because it lacks resources or talent. It is poor where leadership is consumed by personal ambition rather than collective upliftment. In many corridors of power, **leadership has become less about stewardship and more about stockpiling—less about building for the future and more about feasting in the present.**

Ubuntu as the Antidote

Ubuntu teaches that **"I am because we are."** It reminds us that wealth is meaningless when your neighbour is hungry, and power is hollow when it serves only you. It's not merely a moral principle—it's a **governance framework** rooted in humanness, community, and dignity.

Where Ubuntu reigns:
- Leaders serve rather than rule.
- Decisions are made with the whole in mind, not the individual.
- Prosperity is shared, not hoarded.

As one African proverb beautifully puts it:

> "One who eats alone cannot discuss the taste
> of the food with others."

Greed, Democracy, and Leadership

True strength in a state is not found in bloated bureaucracies or dictatorial power.

As **Julius Nyerere** once eloquently said:

> *"To advocate for a strong State is to advocate for a State which… has the power to act on behalf of the people in accordance with their wishes."*

Nyerere called for a democratic, responsive leadership—one that could balance diverse interests, curb conspicuous consumption, and tackle poverty without feeding corruption.

Greed is a destabilizer.

It breeds resentment, erodes trust, and sabotages the very systems meant to serve the people.

It is why public funds are misdirected, why development stagnates, and why even well-meaning governance efforts falter under the weight of self-interest.

We do not need more leaders with swollen appetites.

We need more leaders with enlarged hearts.

Transformative Actions: My Commitment and Contribution

- ≈ I choose to lead with integrity and serve with humility.
- ≈ I will reject greed, hoarding, and selfish ambition.
- ≈ I will honour the principle of Ubuntu by seeking the common good above personal gain.
- ≈ Africa's transformation begins with my choice to live justly, give generously, and lead selflessly.

Now it's your turn:

- In what ways have you witnessed the damage caused by greed in your community or nation?
- How can you embrace Ubuntu in your daily choices and leadership?

NOTES
TRANSFORMATIVE ACTIONS: MY COMMITMENT AND CONTRIBUTION

CHAPTER THIRTY-ONE

SOBER THINKING

Proverb of the Day

"PEOPLE WHO DRINK TO DROWN THEIR SORROWS
SHOULD BE TOLD THAT
SORROW KNOWS HOW TO SWIM."

Sierra Leonean Proverb

Sobriety in Thought and Action

Sober thinking is more than just abstaining from intoxicants.

It is a **deliberate state of clarity**, a **conscious refusal to escape reality**, and a **courageous commitment to confront life with presence and purpose.**

We live in a world where distraction and addiction—be it to substances, screens, status, or habits—have become socially acceptable forms of avoidance.

But what we refuse to face today will return tomorrow in more complex and costly forms.

Africa's transformation depends on a generation that will choose clarity over confusion, discipline over indulgence, and consciousness over chaos.

The Addictive Cycle: More Than Substances

According to psychologist William R. Miller, addiction is not limited to alcohol or drugs.

People can become addicted to any behaviour or activity that gives them temporary pleasure—work, food, relationships, shopping, even worry.

Such compulsions stimulate the brain's reward system, creating euphoric highs that hook us into cycles of dependency.

But over time, these habits **undermine our health, destabilise our families, and distort our destinies.**

In African communities, where young people form the majority, these patterns are particularly dangerous.

The **UN estimates over 28 million drug users in Africa**, rivaling figures in North America.

The crisis is not only one of addiction but of the **absence of systems that support emotional resilience, purpose-driven living, and community healing.**

The Ripple Effect of Escapism

When we fail to think soberly, **we don't just damage ourselves**—we compromise generations after us.

A leader numbed by distraction cannot shape vision.

A parent shackled by addiction cannot model wisdom.

A community overwhelmed by escapism cannot innovate or thrive.

We must reclaim our capacity to think clearly, feel deeply, and act wisely.

A Call to Self-Audit

- What habits have subtly taken control of your daily choices?
- What patterns of behaviour seem harmless, yet consistently sabotage your peace, purpose, and progress?
- What legacy will your current patterns leave for those coming after you?

You are not powerless. Sobriety is possible.

Wholeness is within reach.

And the future depends on your decision today.

Transformative Actions: My Commitment and Contribution

≈ I commit to a life of sober reflection and conscious leadership.
≈ I will identify and confront any patterns in my life that limit my growth or dishonour my calling.
≈ I will model sobriety in thought, speech, and lifestyle—knowing that clarity is the foundation for legacy.

Now it's your turn:

- What addictive patterns do you need to break for the sake of your future and the generations to come?
- In what areas will you choose sobriety—not just of substance, but of thought and spirit?

NOTES
TRANSFORMATIVE ACTIONS: MY COMMITMENT AND CONTRIBUTION

Final Word: A Call to the Sons and Daughters of Africa

This diary was not written to entertain your mind.

It was written to awaken your spirit.

Across these 31 chapters, we have journeyed through proverbs, principles, reflections, and real-life provocations—each one a mirror, a map, and a mandate.

Africa is not waiting for another conference.

She is waiting for her children to **remember who they are**.

To rise beyond limitations of the past, the noise of the present, and the fear of the future.

To steward her wealth—wisdom, land, culture, people, vision—with courage, strategy, and unity.

The cry of the continent is not for perfect leaders, but for **conscious citizens**.

For men and women who will think generationally, speak intentionally, act sacrificially, and love redemptively.

This is not just about nation-building.

This is about soul-building.

Because when the soul of Africa is healed and awakened, the body—her institutions, systems, structures—will follow.

This is your time.

Your moment to disrupt the decay with wisdom.

To silence apathy with action.

To replace convenience with conviction.

Go back to your roots.

Reclaim your wings.

Build as if the next 100 years depend on your next step—because they do.

May the wisdom of our ancestors guide you.
May the fire of purpose sustain you.
And may the God of creation empower you to arise and rebuild.
The journey has only just begun.

About the Author

Cynthia Chirinda is a **Transformation Catalyst**, **Systems Change Practitioner**, and **Personal Development Coach** committed to helping individuals and institutions thrive in purpose-driven alignment. Her work bridges faith, leadership, healing, and nation-building—reaching across boardrooms, grassroots communities, and policy arenas.

Cynthia is the **Founder of Wholeness Incorporated**, a visionary consultancy that provokes critical thinking and champions restorative approaches to personal, organizational, and societal transformation. She is also the **Director of Africa Reform Institute**, empowering citizens to engage in values-based leadership for sustainable development, and the **founder of WOPIZ—Women Politicians' Incubator Zimbabwe**, an initiative committed to mentoring and equipping women for political and public leadership.

With a strong Pan-African worldview and a passion for authentic development, Cynthia has worked extensively in strategy design, team and leadership development, research, communication, and institutional transformation—leveraging over a decade of experience in designing solutions that endure.

Cynthia is a prolific **author**, **coach**, and **public speaker**, whose messages ignite reflection, activate purpose, and cultivate wholeness. Her training expertise spans areas including:

- Transformational Leadership & Strategy Design
- Communication & Executive Presence
- Vitality, Wellness & Balanced Living
- Team Development & Coaching
- Women's Empowerment & Nation Building
- Christian Leadership & Spiritual Exhortation

She is the author of numerous life-shaping books, including:
- The *Connection Factor Series (Personal Growth, Women, Leaders)*
- *Can the Whole Woman Please Stand Up!*
- *Managing Transitions: Navigating Change with Grace*
- *The Whole You—Vital Keys for Balanced Living*
- *Destination Wholeness—Going Beyond Brokenness*
- *You Are Not Damaged Goods series (Reboot and Start Afresh, Blossom and Flourish, Transitioning from Tragedies to Triumph)*
- *Clothed By Love*
- *The Wealthy Diary of African Wisdom*
- *Intelligent Conversations—A Mindset Shift Towards a Developed Africa*
- *Whole Enough to Go: Embracing God's Call in Imperfection*
- Co-authored works:
- *Success Within Reach*
- *Reinvented and Victorious: The Anthology*

She is also the visionary behind:
- **Intelligent Conversations with Cynthia**—A transformational broadcast series focused on leadership, healing, and social development
- **Women Rising in Africa**—A multimedia series spotlighting women trailblazers across the continent
- **The Extra Mile**—A documentary tribute celebrating women nation-builders leading with courage and faith

Cynthia believes that **wholeness is not about perfection—it is about intentionality, truth, and a deep surrender to God's purpose** in every season of life. She continues to use her platforms to incubate transformational leaders, elevate strategic solutions, and co-create the Africa we all want to live in.

Connect with Cynthia:
Website: www.cynthiachirinda.com
Email: info@cynthiachirinda.com
LinkedIn: Cynthia Chirinda

www.ingramcontent.com/pod-product-compliance
Lightning Source LLC
Chambersburg PA
CBHW080412170426
43194CB00015B/2790